Scriptural references pulled from:
https://www.biblegateway.com/versions/Names-of-God-NOG-
Bible/

Written by Matt Cook

Front Cover Artwork by Micah and Noah Cook

Published by
Debarim Publishing, LLC
807 W Broadway
Spiro, OK 74959
www.debarimpublishing.com

This book is dedicated to Keely, Noah, Megan, Shiloh, Chloe, Laramie, Micah, Kendal and the following families: Chafin, Craig, Moudy, Mimms, and Rollmann.

A special thanks to the Pessia, Alfano, Connor, and Ixchu families, Torah Mike and Karen Davidson.

Acknowledgments

I would like to thank the countless men and women who helped me along the way: Jason Keener, Jarrod Bell, Floyd Stumbo, Michael Trinkman, Rob Skiba, David Bedford, and Nema Westmoland.

I would also like to thank Stu Childre and family, Nathan Blackwood and the Blackwood family, the Craig family, the Hagler family, the Fox family, the Wilson family, and Jon and Tracey Horne.

Thank you to Lubbock Christian University, the Church of Christ denomination, Azle ISD, Keller ISD, Fossil Creek Tree Farm, and Canary Cry Radio.

Becoming Jacob

God Hears the Cry of the Fatherless

My mother was the product of a broken home. She had two parents who followed the way of Esau.

In the biblical narrative, Esau was the rightful heir to his father's fortune. He was not interested in his father's ways. He trampled on his lineage by being willing to sell out his birthright over some food.

My grandparent's divorce rippled across the pond of our lives and set off successive ripples of divorce that echoed across the decades. That stopped with me. Through many helpers, Yahuah has helped me turn my lineage from a line of Esaus to Jacobs.

God Calls us All

Yahuah is calling us out of Babylon and into His Kingdom. A Kingdom that is run by Him and not man. We all have a choice. We can choose to be like Jacob and choose the ways of our heavenly father or be like Esau and choose our path. We are all called to Yahuah. He pursues us by using the people around us. We can listen and obey or turn and run.

I grew up in a dysfunctional home with Jacob and Esau examples to follow. I spent much time crying out to Yahuah for an earthly father to show me how to be a man. Ultimately, I had a choice, and fortunately, I chose the path of Jacob. I overcame being fatherless, homeless, living in a broken home, and being orphaned. During it all, the one thing that sustained me was the power of prayer and the belief that Yahuah would send me a father.

Yahuah answered my prayer and delivered it in a powerful way, sending me three father figures at different points in my life.

My faith was developed over many years, which began by leaving religion behind and finding the faith of my family: the faith of Abraham, Isaac, and Jacob—the faith of our fathers. I have been grafted into their family, just like the family that fostered me and gave me a new identity.

There are no natural-born citizens of Yahuah's kingdom. All must be

1

of the second birth or born again.

The Story of Jacob and Esau

When the children inside her were struggling with each other, she said, "If it's like this now, what will become of me?" So she went to ask Yahweh. Yahweh said to her, "Two countries are in your womb. Two nations will go their separate ways from birth. One nation will be stronger than the other, and the older will serve the younger." When the time came for her to give birth, she had twins. The first one born was red. His whole body was covered with hair, so they named him Esau [Hairy]. Afterwards, his brother was born with his hand holding on to Esau's heel, and so he was named Jacob [Heel]. Isaac was 60 years old when they were born. They grew up. Esau became an expert hunter, an outdoorsman. Jacob remained a quiet man, staying around the tents. Gen 25:22-27

Jacob and Esau are two characters you are familiar with from the Bible. In Genesis, it describes them as being twins. Jacob was also called the "Heel Grabber." He had Esau's heel as they were born. The first-born child had the rights and privileges of inheritance. This meant when your father passed away, you inherited everything your father had. The story of Jacob and Esau is an interesting story that is worth diving into.

You see, the two of them were night and day different. The Bible implies that Jacob was about his father's business. He took on the faith of his father, Isaac, and his grandfather, Abraham.

Esau put his confidence in being the firstborn and his abilities. He thought that he would be blessed no matter what. Esau was about Esau. Esau did what he wanted with little regard for his father's forms.

Isaac favored Esau. In some ways, Esau reminded Isaac of himself. As the boys became men, Isaac became advanced in years. Isaac was going blind, and this blindness can be interpreted as physical blindness or spiritual blindness. He had grown blind to the righteousness of Jacob. He loved the traits of self-reliance that Esau developed. He had grown blind to the fact that Esau relied on his strength more than Yahuah's.

Yahuah prompted Rebecca to intervene and picked Jacob to be the primogenitor. (Genesis 25:23) Jacob is the second born, and technically, he wasn't supposed to be able to receive the inheritance by bloodline or by birth. In Yahuah's Kingdom, the second born, or those born again, receive the blessings.

Yahuah is looking for the individual who is seeking Him and pursuing Him. That's who He's making a covenant with. Yahuah, our Father, is seeking people who are seeking Him. The people who seek themselves more than Him, He eventually lets them have whatever they want— searing their conscience with a hot iron, as it tells us in Timothy.

These people will speak lies disguised as truth. Their consciences have been scarred as if branded by a red-hot iron. 1 Timothy 4:2

Jacob is chosen to receive the inheritance. He's chosen because he has the Father's heart. He has his father's desires, which were to follow the Torah, keep His ways, and be a Holy, set-apart people.

For more details, you'll have to read the account in Genesis, but for our story, understand that this Biblical principle exists in the world. If we're like Jacob, we're about our father's business. We do the things that make Him happy. We do the things that He loves. If we are Esau, we do what we want, what seems fun, and whatever makes us happy.

* * *

Both sets of my great-grandparents, the Chafins, and the Hollis, were like Jacob in my family. They loved Yahuah. They pursued Him with all they had. To them, that meant they went to church every time the doors were open: Sunday morning and evening services and Wednesday meetings. They went to all the Sunday school classes. They went to Vacation Bible School, supported gospel meetings, and the missionaries. They were always there to encourage brethren. They set an example for their children.

The other side of my family, the Hollis family, was incredibly old school. They were so old school that in the 1980s, they still did not have an indoor laundry room. She washed her clothes outside and dried them on a clothesline. Not only did she wash them outside, but she also washed them outside with a 1950 washing machine with an electric ringer on the top. Her laundry room was the backyard because she would hook up a water hose to it.

The Hollis family went every time the church doors were open. They pursued Yahuah and loved being at church. It was a part of who they were. They were friendly, kind, simple folks who weren't trying to make waves, make a statement, or cause problems. They just wanted to live a quiet, simple life.

My grandmother, on the other hand, was more like Esau. My Granny Marge did what she wanted. She grew up in a small town with very conservative parents who lived a very simple life. She went to the big city of Lubbock, got into the medical field as a nurse, and started hanging around the nurses, doctors, and medical facilities. She decided that she liked pursuing power and money more than she did pursuing the things of Yahuah. She, too, was like Esau. She did what she wanted. She married multiple times after divorcing my grandfather. Granny Marge lived a train wreck life and left her children to deal with the consequences.

This story of Jacob and Esau lives out today. It can be in anyone's family. What are you going to do? Live like Jacob or like Esau?

How Firm a Foundation

To better understand my family history, we have to start with my great-grandparents, Carl and Frances Chafin of Knox City, Texas.

Carl was one of seven children in a blended family. We don't know much about Carl's birth father, but his stepfather was known to be a drunk. Being the oldest, he had to step up early and care for his brothers and sisters. Growing up in the Great Depression, Carl learned to be tough and self-reliant. He learned to be a "Jack of all Trades" and did everything from flipping hamburgers to farming. Carl did whatever he could to keep food on the table for his family.

At some point, he took on a job at a hamburger stand. He shared the stand with a blind man who was the main cook. Carl took the orders and the cash, and the blind man cooked all the burgers. As a child, I never questioned the validity of his story, but as an adult, I have so many questions about how such a thing would work.

Along the way, he met my great-grandmother Frances. As a young girl, Frances was not able to pronounce her name. Everyone in the family would call her Frankie. Frances couldn't say Frankie but instead said, "Hanky." The name stuck with her for the rest of her life. She became known as Hank. Yes, I had a great-grandmother named Hank.

Hank grew up quite a bit different than her husband, Carl. Hank had a father who was a spiritual leader in the church. She grew up going to church every time the doors were open and had a great love of the Bible.

When Hank was a teenager and Carl was still just a young man in his twenties, they knew they wanted to make a life together. Carl knew that Hank was serious about her faith, and he knew that if he were going to be with her, he would have to study the word. He would learn how to be a godly man.

Hank and Carl began a beautiful life together, farming in West Texas. They farmed with family. Hank's sister married one of Carl's step-brothers. They lived near each other and shared farming duties on nearby properties. They worked the land on a lease-to-buy option. Eventually, they earned enough money to buy some of the property. They met great friends who shouldered the task and responsibility along the way. Farming was much more labor-intensive back in the Great Depression. Farms relied on lots of people to make the work easy and quick. This meant everyone you knew, friends and family, would help you do the job. It's a concept in Texas that we call "Neighboring."

When Hank and Carl got married, they did not have much money. Their family helped them purchase a house that was initially the bunkhouse on the Bush Burnett Ranch. This old bunkhouse had been removed and reassembled on the new home site in Knox City. This farmhouse was built out of old wood in the 1930s. They rebuilt it to save as much of the old wood as possible. This is the house where they would raise all three children and live out their lives. The house is still there today as of the writing in 2023.

Hank and Carl raised three children together on their remote family farm. They were free from the hustle and bustle of everyday city life. Hank and Carl ran the farm together, answering only to each other. The whole family worked on the farm for the common good.

When Hank would help chop cotton (removing weeds), she would leave one of the kids at the end of the row while she made a round. A round consisted of going to the end of the row and returning to where you started. Each time she made a round, she would check on the child and move them to the next row. No daycare was available on the farm, and the work needed to be done.

This was also very equitable work, with the men and women sharing responsibilities. Hank would work in the field all day, and she would help put food on the table at night. It wasn't her doing all the household chores. They didn't work that way. Carl would help fold the laundry and make the beds. He did not deem that work to be beneath him. One time, I commented that housework was "for women!" He was not impressed by this statement, and he dropped his schedule for the day and had me do housework with him. I learned quickly that Carl did not see life tasks as female or male. We work together and do what needs to be done.

Hank was no stranger to demanding work. She worked as hard or harder than many men of that day. There is a story of Hank working a hay baler with her friend. This was before modern machinery and many moving parts that made automation possible. Many machines, like bailers, were operated manually using your body weight as leverage to move the parts connected to the handle. This lever is what was used to compress a bale.

One afternoon, as the kids came home on the school bus, they saw a couple of old ladies giving all they had to compress a bale. In full view of everyone on the school bus, they saw their mother and their friend's mother wrestling with this hay baler out in the field. The entire bus thought seeing these old ladies working this hay baler alone was hilarious.

Hard work was in Hank and Carl's DNA. It was in everyone's DNA at that time in US history. Many of you also have grandparents with comparable stories of how difficult their life was and how hard they had to work to put food on the table.

This was a wonderful time in modern US history when many families were together all day. They worked and played together. To accommodate the farm families, schools took extra long winter breaks to allow the children to help harvest the cotton crop. Some members of modern society might become disgusted at the thought of this "child labor." I consider this beautiful and something I long to recreate in my family.

Hank and Carl had three children: my grandfather, Henry Chafin, and my two great aunts, Ann Chafin and Jo Chafin.

Building on the Sand

Henry Chafin, my grandfather, was the oldest and only son in the family. Like many only sons, sometimes he made it hard for others to walk in his footsteps. In his parent's eyes, Henry was the family's young patriarch and could almost do no wrong.

Henry went to high school in Knox City. After graduation, he decided to be the first one in the family to go to college. Henry chose Texas Tech University in Lubbock, Texas. While attending Texas Tech, he would go home in the summers and off periods and still help with work on the farm. Henry had grown up in Knox City and had only known small-town life. Now, he was in the big city, full of choices and options he had never considered or heard.

While at Tech, he had several atheist professors who taught evolution. Henry had grown up attending church, which caused great conflict in his mind. He heard his professors say one thing, but he had heard his Bible class teachers say something different about how the earth was made. With the conflict, Henry reasoned that his Bible class teachers must have been wrong. What could they know, being from a small town, Knox City? Henry decided that the scientists were right and pursued science over faith.

The sad part of Henry's life is that he never returned to his parent's faith. He bought the lie of Evolution. Henry dropped everything he was taught and became Agnostic, finding a new faith in man. This is part of the story where he chooses Esau's life over Jacob's.

Meanwhile, his parents were still deeply rooted in their faith and were at church whenever the doors opened. Carl was a teacher and elder, and Hank also helped teach Bible classes. They were active in all aspects of the church and knew everyone there. They lived the life of Jacob.

Ann was the middle child in the Chafin family. She was a young, red-haired girl with lots of passion and vigor for life. Ann loved her parents deeply. She sat at the feet of her parent's teaching. She listened and learned. Ann never departed from the truth that her parents taught her. Ann grew up among a faithful congregation that loved Yahuah and loved each other like family.

Ann spent her entire life in the same farmhouse where her parents lived. She also spent her whole life in the church her parents attended. After high school, Ann went to college to become a teacher. She taught school for a few years away from home. When she came home during the summers, she noticed how much her parents were aging. She knew that they needed more help. Ann began spending all of her free time helping with the farm work.

Jo, like Ann, was another representation of Jacob. Jo never lost her faith and was faithfully married for over fifty years. Ann and Jo lived a very different life than that of their brother.

Choosing the Life of Esau

Time marches on, and there is a widening chasm between what happens to Ann and Jo versus what happens to Henry. Henry goes on to marry a young nurse named Margie. Margie rejected her faith after attending college choosing the life of Esau like Henry.

What seemed to be a match made in heaven was a recipe for disaster. The marriage couldn't survive with two Easu's. Before they divorced, Henry and Margie had three children, Stan, Dorothy (my mother), and Donna.

After the two "Esau's" figured out this was not working for either of them, they each took remarkably similar paths. They both had multiple marriages and life partners, none of which had a happy ending.

After the divorce, Henry was drawn to the mountains and decided he wanted to be a mountain man. He was the founder of a hunting lodge in southwestern Colorado. He remarried, giving his kids a stepmother. The three children follow him to Colorado. Being in this blended family was difficult for Stan, Dorothy, and Donna. Their stepmother was not always kind. She was especially unkind to Dorothy. My mother had many bitter memories of being raised by her unloving step-mom.

Margie stayed in Lubbock. She took advantage of the high society circle that she found herself in, working for the hospital. Margie enjoyed the social life and liked being among the movers and shakers.

Doing the Best they Could

My mother grew up in the sixties, and like many of her peers, she became interested in drugs and Rock 'N Roll. My mother went on wild adventures with her brother and sister. Stan, Dorothy, and Donna were three lost kids trying to find their way in the early 1970s. As they moved from childhood to adulthood the tight bond they had continued, and they weren't ready to go their separate ways.

Stan was the first one of them to get a job. Dorothy and Donna had nothing tying them down, so they tagged along with Stan. He had gotten a job in Odessa, Texas, as a metal fabricator. He would be welding in the Permian Basin oilfield. While in Odessa, all three would fall in love and marry.

My mother, Dorothy, met a hardworking welder who was from Odessa. Steve was a young man who dropped out of high school before he learned to read and write. He was seventeen, welding professionally in the oilfield, and was already considered one of the best at his specific skill set. My mother was a year older than him. They fell in love and decided that they had to get married.

The life of a welder/fabricator is a nomadic lifestyle. The oil industry goes up and down. The discovery of new oil fields and better technologies move resources and people worldwide. Steve had to chase the oil field across the US.

* * *

Shortly after my parent's weekend honeymoon, my dad got a job in Kilgore, Texas. A few months later, I entered the world in the middle of the oil patch in Kilgore, Texas. The first four years of my life were full of moving from one opportunity to another. We moved all over North America, searching for work in the oil and gas industry. We lived in North Dakota, Wyoming, Kansas, and Oklahoma. When I was old enough to start preschool, we settled back in Odessa. We bought a trailer living on the same property that Nanny lived on. The young couple didn't know much about raising me, and having a grandmother nearby was helpful.

Secret Lives and Abuse

My father came from an Esau-type life as well. This upbringing shaped him into who he was and ultimately led to issues within our family. One of the most prominent individuals who caused problems for our family was Steve's dad, Leon. Leon had another life that few of us knew about. He was always away with something work-related. He was known to have women on the side. One such night, he was with a prostitute. When he woke up, she was not there. She left, taking his clothes, car, and wallet. He was desperate and called my uncle, Stan, to be rescued. My uncle had to bring him a set of clothes and return him home. No one in the family knew of his secret life except for my uncle.

Leon was, unfortunately, a 32nd-degree Freemason. This is something that I have denounced, and I have asked for the cleansing blood of Yeshua to wash over my descendants.

One of the things you often see in the Masonic lines is child sexual abuse and the death of the firstborn son. Leon's oldest son died of cancer at 36, and his children passed on the abuse they had experienced to me and my youngest cousin.

Steve's brother Jackie had two sons. These two boys had created an underground clubhouse. It was very small, and no adults could crawl in to check on the clubhouse. Once you were in the clubhouse, you were safe from the eyes of any adults. At first, I thought this was

16

amazing. Soon, it became a club of horrors for me. The oldest brother would carry out sexual assaults on his cousins, myself included.

I was only in kindergarten at the time. It would be much later in life before I realized what had happened to me. I have realized that these young boys must have had someone abusing them. They were acting out on what had been done to them.

Growing up in a Trailer Park

My dad was barely out of his teens when I was young and didn't always have the best judgment. They say a man's brain does not completely develop until age twenty-five. A good father doesn't tear down his kids. He is patient, loving, and kind to them. He seeks their best interest and strives to drive out fear, worry, and doubt. He builds confidence in his children. However, that was my dad.

Fathers, don't make your children bitter about life. Ephesians 6:4

I was terrified of thunderstorms. It wasn't the lightning so much, but the sound of the thunder that terrified me. My dad thought it was fun to aggravate me. If I was playing outside when a thunderstorm hit, I would run back home as fast as I could. My dad would lock me outside the house and not let me in. I remember having a panic attack at the back door because I thought lightning would strike me. To this day, I am still a little jumpy when a thunderstorm hits.

When I was in kindergarten, my dad decided I was old enough to learn a new trick. He showed me how to douse my hand in lighter fluid and ignite it without burning it. After the fuel burned up, it was easy to extinguish. He could safely extinguish the flames and didn't get burned.

The day after he showed that to me, he conveniently left out the lighter fluid and the lighter. When my mom wasn't looking, I entered their bedroom, covered my hand with lighter fluid, and set it on fire.

I can remember seeing the flames shoot off my hand. I started to flail my arm in the air, which only fanned the flames higher and higher with each frantic wave. I began to scream as I ran towards my mother. She met me halfway through the house, screaming, "Oh my god! I can't believe you did this!" She quickly put out the flame and called for help.

The next thing I knew, I was in the emergency room being treated for second-degree burns. I still have the scars today.

One of my earliest school memories is playing in the dirt with a kid I had met on the school bus. We were bored with nothing to do on the summer day, and I conceived a terrible idea. I told the boy, "Why don't we take this dirt and fill the neighbor's car with sand." (Not inside the car but inside the gas tank.) He said, "It seems like fun to me."

The next day, the neighbor tried to start his car, and of course, it would not start. He started trying to figure out what was wrong with his vehicle. As you can imagine, young boys are not very good at being sneaky or covering up their tracks. We left a trail of sand from his car to where we were playing. It was apparent who committed the crime.

Later in the evening, I heard a loud pounding on the door. I peeked through the curtains only to see this angry man with veins bulging on his neck and forehead. My mother was home alone while my dad worked in the oil field. I was no dummy, and I turned around and slinked off back to my room like nothing had happened. She let him in, and he began to go on a tirade for the next fifteen minutes, yelling at my mom. He told her, "Your son ruined my new car by filling it with sand. I demand that you pay my repair bill!" Unfortunately for him, we had no money to pay for his new engine.

Throughout their marriage my parents needed extra income. Like many women in the 1970s, my mother began to sell Avon to earn the extra money we needed. Sometimes, she would have to take me with her because I was too young to stay home alone.

While she would be with a client, she would make me stay in the car. I got bored fast and was mad that my mother had taken me on her ridiculous sales calls. My perspective was minimal, and I had no idea the pressures that my mom must have been under trying to support our family. I was very inconsiderate of what was going on in her life.

While waiting in the car, I grew restless and wanted something to do. I had seen my dad change the spark plugs in the car recently. I watched him and learned the wires could easily be pulled off the spark plugs. I thought I could help my dad with the vehicle's maintenance. I stuck my hand under the dash and pulled the hood release. I went around the front of the car, opened the hood, and removed the wires to help the car "run better." After pulling all the wires, I ran out of mechanical knowledge and got bored staring at the engine. I closed the hood and jumped back in the car, fearing she might return any minute.

When my mother did return, the car wouldn't start. She said, "That's weird?" Then she looked at my nervous, non-poker face and knew what happened. She popped open the hood to take a look. She yelled, "Matthew Doyle Cook, what have you done to my car!" I sheepishly grinned and tried to turn on all the boyhood charm I could muster. It was no use. I had done it. I was in trouble!

She was forced to go back and knock on the client's door and asked to use the phone. She called my dad. Thirty minutes later, he showed up. He was not happy with me. I'm sure I had the beating of my life after that event! He finally did get the car to run again after another day of working on it.

I don't remember going on more Avon sales calls with my mom afterward.

* * *

Even with the additional income of Avon, my parents were on a road headed for disaster. They were living in poverty and were ill-equipped for life, much less parenting. Most importantly, they didn't have the word of Yahuah in their hearts or minds. They were not doing anything to work on their faith.

It became increasingly difficult for this young couple. With all the stressors, they began to fight and argue over everything. One day, I was told to load up in the car. Mom told me we were going to go away for a while. I was excited. I didn't know what she meant.

My last childhood memory of my dad is me standing in the car's back seat, waving goodbye to him, and seeing the tears run down his cheeks. He was waving goodbye to his wife and child, who would never return. My mom left my dad with a tank full of gas and headed to Knox City to the Chafin homestead.

Headed to the Farm

My mother and her siblings had been blessed with two role models. The Chafins and the Hollis' would be the only constant force of good in their lives. The Chafins strived to build a relationship with their three grandchildren. They would call, write, and send money often. They wanted to wield a Jacob-like influence on their grandchildren.

Hank and Carl wanted their grandkids to grow up as faithful, Bible-believing people. They were saddened by their grandchildren's lifestyle choices but held out hope that a difference could be made in my life.

Hank and Carl happily married for thirty-plus years and loved each other dearly. They were living the "American Dream" and had a piece of land to call their own. The land was now providing a living.

When my mother and I arrived after leaving my father, my grandparents met my mother and I at the door with smiles and open arms. I have never felt a hug as warm and kind as their hug that day. I can still remember how loved it made me feel. I knew I was home. I was excited to be there with my favorite people. They helped my mom get a new job and a new car.

I was as happy as could be. I finally got to be around a godly man. Grandpa loved spending time with me. He was willing to teach me at every opportunity that was provided. No drama. No fuss. He wasn't crazy, didn't cuss, drink, or have a bad temper. I spent every waking moment with him. If he went out in the field and grabbed a shovel, I went out and grabbed a shovel. If he put on a hat, I put on a hat. If he put on his boots, I put on boots. If he wore a green shirt, I wore a green shirt. I wanted to do everything like him. I tried to mimic him in every way. I knew he was a good man.

Mom was happy as well. She knew Hank and Carl loved her dearly and only wanted the best for us. They were hoping to help my mother establish order from the life of chaos that she had created. They even had us going to church with them. This was no easy task since they were "every time the doors were open" kind of folks.

In the twenty-sixth chapter of the book of Jasher, there is an account of Abraham at the end of his life setting up a traveler's oasis to help the travelers along the way. I like to picture him setting up the world's first truck stop. Abraham is known to all for his generosity and hospitality. The Chafins modeled a life like Abraham. They had opened their doors to their "prodigal granddaughter" returning home.

There was great rejoicing over her coming back home. They were sad about the circumstances of the visit but never let that be shown. I look fondly upon this time in my young life. It was my first glimpse of "heaven on earth." It is much like what I imagine it will be like when we are reunited with our Maker in the second coming.

Making Bad Choices

The Chafins crafted a structured environment filled with work, family, and church attendance. They were sewing seeds of the kingdom in my mother's life. Before long, my mom grew restless though. She wanted more fun in her life. She began to look for other young men in the area to be friends with. My mom found some men who were interested in smoking pot with her. She was choosing to reject the faith of her grandparents and seek her path again.

The choice to have a fun lifestyle was soon to catch up with my mom. My mom had parked her car in the driveway behind Ann's car. Ann had to move the car. When she did, she noticed my mom had been smoking pot in it. Ann alerted her parents. They soon had a "come to Jesus meeting" with my mom. Giving her an ultimatum, "If you can't clean up your act, then we're not going to provide this car for you, and we're not going to be able to help you!" My mom refused to change. She departed from Jacob's path and returned to Esau's path.

We got kicked out of the only stability that my mother had ever known. Once again, we found ourselves homeless. Kicking us out was one of the hardest things Hank and Carl ever did. They loved the time they had with my mom and me.

We hopped in the car and headed toward the Hollis farm. It was less than fifteen minutes from the Chafin farm. My great-grandfather Hollis was a blacksmith and a farmer. On his farm, a windmill supplied all their drinking water. That windmill was the coldest and best-tasting water I have ever had. He was a man of few words. I liked spending time with him, but he was not as patient and kind as my great-grandfather Carl.

The Hollis were more hands-off with their children. They provided very little structure to their children and grandchildren. I always felt closer to the Chafins than the Hollis family. It was very similar to a blended family. One family is the "fun parent," and the other parent is the one that makes the kid "tow the line." The Hollis were the "fun parents". You could do whatever you wanted with minimal questions asked. The Chafins, on the other hand, wanted to know your plan and what you were up to.

Going to first grade in Knox City, Texas, was a big change from the much larger schools in Odessa. Knox City is the kind of place that has one blinking light at the intersection. The entire elementary school, jr. high, high school, and administrative offices were inside a few city blocks. My first-grade teacher, Ms. Klements, was a sweet, old lady to anyone not in her class. She had been teaching for a long time and was a legend in that community. She was in her last year of teaching and only had one thing on her mind: how to get to the end of the year so she could live her best life.

She seemed as if she was one hundred years old. I thought, "This lady doesn't even know if I'm here. I have to go find my mom!" I was mourning the loss of my family unit the way I had known it. In time, my mourning had changed to anger. All I wanted to do was return to an intact, godly family. I wanted my parents to make it work. I was mad at the world. I just wanted to be with mom. So, I decided to ditch school.

These classrooms had an outside entry that led to a portico. Once I breached the classroom door, I was outside. I was bound and determined to be reunited with my mom. I ran out of that school building and wandered the streets of Knox City until I found her. It seemed like a mile away, but as an adult, I went back to show my children where the school was in relation to where my mother worked, and it turns out it's only a few blocks!

I found the office my mother worked in. When I entered the front door, the adults looked at me like, "Oh my! What is this child doing here? He's supposed to be at school!" I don't fully remember that moment. I was crying and upset, looking for my mother. They quickly helped reunite me with her. She burst into tears seeing the anguish on my face, knowing full well she had been partly to blame for the pain I was experiencing. She held me tight and comforted me as she took me back to the Hollis farm. She spent the rest of the day playing with me in my room and talking to me.

This is when I began to long for a father. I began to pray that Yahuah would make it right for me and my family. I prayed He would restore my family and give me an intact family. I longed for my mom to become a God-fearing woman. I wanted a father who had the Lord first in his life and his family second. This would be my heart's desire for the coming years.

Little did I know that I longed for the same things Jacob wanted. We both longed for being about the will of our Heavenly Father. No doubt it is in Yahuah's will for a child to grow up with a father. If a fatherless child prays for a father, there is no doubt He will answer that prayer.

My mother did not feel fulfilled at her job in Knox City, and she realized she would need more training to provide a better life for the two of us. She was tired of being a homeless single mother. She wanted to move to a bigger city. She thought Lubbock would provide more opportunities for her to work and attend college.

She called up Granny Marge who had recently settled down with a decent man. She was done sowing her wild oats and was now in a stable situation. She told my mom, "Hey, you should come here to Lubbock and live with me and your step-dad, Bill."

We went from living in Esau's house to Jacob's house with the Chafins and the Hollis. Now, we were returning to Esau's house. Yahuah had her in a wonderful place to get spiritual nourishment, to be loved on, and financially set on her feet. He had her set up for a Jacob life, which she rejected.

Papa Bill

Papa Bill had a trailer house on a few acres of land. He had retired from the Navy and had a second career in the welding and machining industry. He had his own slice of the American Dream. He had a home, acreage, and a shop.

He lived off a government pension and dabbled with some side income streams. Papa Bill loved animals. We raised goats that needed to be milked daily. I grew to love the taste of their sweet milk. He also had a birdhouse full of exotic birds that he sold to pet stores and the flea market.

Papa Bill knew that I didn't have a father in my life. He did his best to teach me how to be a man. He was gruff and direct. One morning before his first drink, he decided I needed a pony. He asked me, "Would you like a pony, Matt?" It is a universal truth across all income levels and nationalities that when asking a 7-year-old, "Do you want your pony?" they will all say "YES!"

One of Bill's requirements is that "If you're going to ride this pony, you must capture this "Wild Mustang" and put a saddle and bridle on her. You will be the first one to ride her. She's going to buck you off. I will show you how to train her." Papa Bill showed me how to saddle and bridle a horse.

He taught me how to care for her and let her know who her boss was.

One of the first things I had to learn was how to catch her. Keeping a pocket full of sugar cubes was a great trick. She'd come running! Naturally, I named her Sugar because she came running up for the sugar cubes. Once we were both comfortable, it was time to get on her. He would explain how the Natives would ride horses bareback. "Only the toughest cowboys could ride bareback," he once said. He had me get on her only to be bounced right off. "Boy, you have to get back up on her, don't let her win!" I did that several times and was able to get on her bareback and ride her around without getting bucked off. To which he said, "It's time. You are both ready!"

I was a full-on cowboy! He let me begin to ride her every day with one condition: I had to do it all. Keep in mind this is a Shetland pony, not a full-sized horse, but when you're seven, and you have a pony, it's a real horse.

I would get off the school bus daily, change clothes, grab my cowboy hat, and catch my horse. I would saddle her and go wherever I wanted to go. I wore Spurs, a cowboy hat, and a pearl snap shirt. I thought of myself as a real cowboy. I gained tremendous confidence. There was not anything I couldn't do, so I thought.

Papa Bill had a two-acre parcel on the end of a private dirt road. It felt like we were in the country but on the edge of a trailer park. I rode Sugar up the road every day. In the park, there were some girls I got to know on the bus. Every day, they whined to me and asked, "Can we please ride Sugar? We just want to ride her!"

I was out riding, and they continued to beg and said things like, "We have never ridden a pony!" I felt sorry for them and gave in. I said, "Sure. You can ride Sugar." The girls hopped on, and they rode Sugar for a few minutes. I grew angry and impatient. It didn't take me long to shout out, "Times up! Time to get off. The show is over. This is my pony. I want her back."

In fairness to them, they had just gotten on the pony, and I immediately told them, "It's time to get off!" I was ridiculous.

* * *

They laughed at me and said, "Silly boy, we're not getting off this pony. We just got on her!"

My anger and my blood began to boil. My face turned red. I began to shout and cuss. They refused to listen and obey my directives. I didn't have much control over the direction my life took. I wanted to be more in control of my destiny. When someone didn't listen to me and seemed to laugh at me and mock me, my anger would grow even hotter.

These girls thought it was funny to see me get angry. They were in no hurry to get off my pony. They weren't about to give up quickly. They just laughed and had a wonderful time.

I did what came naturally. I picked up a rock and I hurled it in their direction. With all the accuracy I could muster, I threw that rock as hard and far as possible. Like David's rock when he fell Goliath, my rock hit right on the spot. It hit the little girl who had asked to ride the horse. Immediately, it ripped open her skin, and blood began to spill all over her face, down her shirt, and on the horse. Both girls burst into tears and jumped off the horse.

I said, "It's about time you got off my horse!" I grabbed the reins of my horse, and I continued my day, doing what I wanted to do. Eventually, I rode back home and put her up for the night. After rubbing her down and feeding her sugar cubes, I came inside in time for dinner and homework. It seemed just like a typical day for me—no big deal. Of course, I didn't say anything about what had happened. I went straight to my room as if nothing had ever happened.

As sunset approached, there was a loud knocking at the door. This was just like when I had filled the gas tank with sand. Papa Bill let the man in and listened to the man go on a crazy rant, yelling, screaming, and cursing. He told them he had to rush his little girl to the emergency room to get stitches. They demanded an apology and help with the medical bills.

* * *

My grandmother was horrified that her sweet little grandchild could do such a horrible thing to a little girl. She immediately thought she would have me apologize for my terrible behavior. She entered my room and said, "You must come out and apologize to the parents and the girl. Come out here and apologize now!" I looked at her with a cold, hard, death stare and replied,"No! I'm not apologizing. I am not sorry one bit for what I did. I told the girl to get off my horse. She didn't listen to me. I don't care what happened to her. She got what she deserved. I'm not saying anything to them!"

Amazingly, I didn't get punished for my behavior. I guess that's what happens when you live with your grandparents. They're not supposed to be the disciplinarians in your life.

The young girl recovered and was on the school bus the next day. Our relationship was never the same.

Papa Bill lived with chronic back pain and self-medicated with alcohol. He started drinking when he woke up, and he would drink until he passed out on the couch around midday. This was his typical day. I'm no expert here, but I'm sure he was a full-on alcoholic.

Papa Bill also was not receptive to neighbor dogs. We had birds, rabbits, goats, and dogs that we were selling. Stray dogs would often wander up and chase our animals. This caused them to get stressed and jump fences. Bill was not a fan. He made it clear when he put up the sign: Keep your stray animals out of my property. If you can't keep your animal off my property, I will shoot it.

Everybody knew he was serious about keeping his property free from unwanted animals. On more than one occasion, I remember seeing him raise a gun and shoot a dog at a full sprint across his pasture. He would drop it, dig a hole the next day with the tractor, and bury the dead dog. He didn't care whose dog it was.

One day, I was outside playing in a kiddie pool. It was the cheap plastic kind with a rigid shell. It was twelve inches deep and maybe four feet across. It was great fun on a sweltering summer day. My grandmother, Margie, sat next to me in her chair and read a book.

Granny Marge had nodded off while she was reading her book. She awoke to the sound of the yapping dog and a dreadful realization of what would happen. She knew that Papa Bill, even though he was passed out on the couch, would hear this dog and would come out with a gun ready.

Sure enough, while I was enjoying the warm sunny day with a dog to play with, I heard the back door creak. I saw Papa Bill with the rifle pointed at me and the dog. Bill had his sights on the dog, who was now about three feet away from me, and he squeezed the trigger and dropped the dog dead in the pool right next to me. My delightful day came instantly crashing to a halt. I now find myself surrounded by a pool of blood. My ears were ringing, and everything was a blur. Granny Marge pulled me out of the pool and ensured I was okay. She was horrified and was yelling at Bill. "I can't believe you just did that! You could have killed Matt!"

Gabe

My mother enrolled in a business college to beef up her resume so she could work in an office. When she wasn't going to school, she was working at Pinky's Liquor Store to save up for our own place.

Since she was working, I rode a bus every day to school. The school was about a 20-minute, one-way bus ride on rough country roads.

It was understood that "cool kids" sat in the back of the bus, and no one else could sit back there without being one of them. If you tried, you would be bullied and harassed the entire ride to school.

I was a spunky little kid who didn't take crap from anybody. I got tired of how those kids acted. They made fun of everybody, and I did not like being made fun of. One day, they were unmercifully picking on me. I remember being so fed up with them that I was determined to take revenge. I worked up a big loogie, spun around, and spit that loogie as hard as I could across the school bus. Just as I did, one of the nicest high school kids on the bus stood up just in time for my spit to land on her face. She was the last one that I wanted mad at me because she defended the defenseless kids on the bus. As she wiped off my loogie from her face, she turned around and yelled at the older kids. She said, "It's your fault this happened!" A hush fell over the bus just in time for my stop. I walked off the bus feeling proud of my new found friend. The bus was different for me after that. Those kids left me alone.

After stopping at my trailer, the bus rambled on another couple of miles to a little farmhouse. There, it picked up a little red-haired kid with noticeable features. He had a little sister with him that was extremely sweet and incredibly quiet. She stayed with her brother for protection.

Gabe and Robyn were toward the end of the route. The bus was full, and many times our bus driver, Rusty, was in a hurry so we wouldn't be late to school. As Gabe and Robyn walked down the crowded aisle, Rusty would start creeping the bus forward, sending a message, "Hey, kids, you better sit down because I'm ready to go!"

I had watched Gabe and Robyn before and felt compassion for them. Gabe was one year younger than me, and his sister had just started kindergarten. Gabe got picked on because of his red hair and striking features. He became an easy target for ear-thumping.

I could tell that Gabe and Robyn came from a loving home. They looked like they had it all together. I was jealous of what they had. I had few friends and hoped to find a friend who liked playing in the dirt with tractors. This day was the day that turned my life around.

I decided to let Gabe and Robyn sit with me on the bus. Gabe and I began to talk. Quickly, I start asking Gabe a million questions. Who are you? What do you like to do? Tell me about your mom and dad.

To my amazement, I discovered that Gabe lived on a working farm. I also found out that Gabe played with toy tractors, loved farm life, and wanted to be a farmer. To which I exclaimed, "Me too!" Within seconds, we both knew that we had found a kindred spirit. There are no coincidences in the Kingdom.

The bus driver and the bullies on the school bus were all "pots of special purpose" in Yahuah's hands as He masterfully wove the hearts of two small boys together that day.

* * *

You may ask me, "Why does God still find fault with anyone? Who can resist whatever God wants to do?" Who do you think you are to talk back to God like that? Can an object that was made say to its maker, "Why did you make me like this?" 21 A potter has the right to do whatever he wants with his clay. He can make something for a special occasion or something for everyday use from the same lump of clay. Romans 9:19-21

By the end of the twenty-minute ride to school, we had gone from perfect strangers to instant best friends. I told Gabe about my grandfather, working on the farm, and how much I loved the farm. We both shared our desire to be farmers. We didn't take long to figure out that we both had a toy tractor collection, and we loved to play for hours on end with our toy tractors. We both loved to pretend that we were farming.

Thanks to Papa Bill, I had my "own wheels" with my pony Sugar. I took the first opportunity I had to ride to Gabe's house. It seems like it happened the same day, but I'm unsure if it occurred in the same week. I came home from school and did my homework and chores. It was just one of those perfect days where the temperature was in the 70s and the sky was bright blue and full of sunshine. Not a cloud in the sky. So, as soon as I changed into my play clothes, I went and caught Sugar, saddled her up, and headed out to Gabe's. My grandmother said, "Matt, be home by sunset!" To which I said, "Okay."

Mr. Moudy, Where can I put my horse?

Gabe's house was about two miles from our home. As a kid, that seemed like a long distance to ride my horse. I loved the adventure and felt very grown up. I was a cowboy in my mind.

I rode to the farm in my pearl snap shirt, hat, and spurs. I dismounted from Sugar and walked up to Gabe's dad, Mr. Moudy, shook his hand, looked him in the eye, and said, "Mr. Moudy, I've got this horse, Sugar, here, and I need a place to put her. I've come here to play with Gabe. Where can I put her?"

Mr. Moudy was impressed by my confidence, firm handshake, and how I talked to him. He was laughing on the inside. He thought, "Wow, somebody has worked with this boy. He is different." Still, to this day, it's one of his favorite stories of how we first met. Mr. Moudy quickly showed me a small horse stall. I walked her into the pen, where I turned her loose, and then I ran over to where Gabe was playing as fast as I could. Gabe was playing with his toy tractors in the dirt. I knew what to do and jumped right in.

For the first time in our lives, we found another person who was serious about playing with tractors. We played like we were working. We were both serious about farming the right way. We wanted our farms to be exactly like what we saw in the fields around us and the farming magazines that we idolized. We weren't into breaking and destroying our toy tractors or trying to crash them. We were serious about treating them as if they were real tractors on a real farm and we were making real crops.

As the sun set, I gathered up my things and headed home. As soon as we turned towards home, Sugar started to run at full speed, anticipating the sugar cubes she would soon receive. I felt like the good guy in the movie riding off into the sunset.

From time to time, we all have these defining moments that change our destiny. They impact everything you do. Alvin and I both know that this day changed us forever. He met a little boy who needed guidance, love, and attention. I had met the man I had been praying for. This was a divine appointment from our Heavenly Father. At the same time, I knew that I had found the perfect friend in Gabe.

God had moved the Moudys from Canyon, Texas, to Lubbock, Texas, for a job, so they thought. Looking back now, they know that God had worked to set up this very moment in time and place to meet me. His intention was for me to meet the Moudys, and He knew it would progress with perfect timing.

Years before, Alvin was moving out of his farmhouse. He was forced to quit farming and move into town. He was upset about having to do this and just was in a funk. While they were moving, the spirit prompted him to go into the house again. As he entered the house, the phone was ringing. He picked it up, and a man on the other end of the line was offering him a salary job to farm. It was an answer to his prayer and a path for him to move forward doing the thing he loved. Only later did I realize that the reason for the phone call was to meet me.

I knew I was in the presence of my people. These were the people I had been looking for. These were the kind of people that walked in the way of Jacob.

Matt's Family Tree

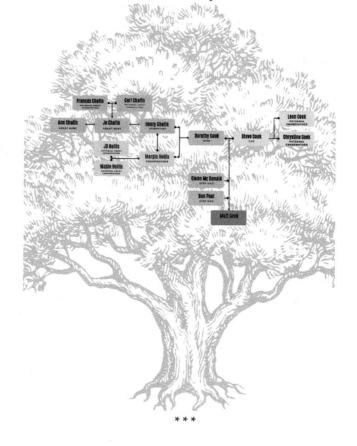

* * *

Left to right- Jo, Ann, and Henry Chaffin

Carl & Hank- Knox City, TX

* * *

Granny Marge & Gramps- Knox City, TX

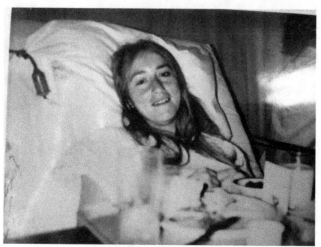

Mom on my birth date- Kilgore, TX

* * *

Matt with lighter fluid burn- Kilgore, TX

Carl, Hank, and Matt- Knox City, TX

* * *

Matt and his mom after a day of fishing- Lubbock, TX

Matt and Gabe- Lubbock, TX

* * *

Matt and Sugar

Sugar, Robyn, Gabe, and Matt- Lubbock, TX

* * *

Robyn, Gabe, and Matt- Panhandle Water Slide

Matt, Gabe, and Lynsey

* * *

Matt, Donna, Mom, and Granny Marge

Matt and Keely- Wedding Rehearsal

* * *

Back Row- Alan Craig and Charlie Green
Middle Row- Kerri Craig, Keely, and Matt
Front Row- Lindsay Craig

Back Row- Noah, Micah, and Alan
Front Row- Kendal, Kerri, Chloe, Laramie, Keely, Matt, Shiloh, and
Megan

Going to Church

Throughout second and third grade, I was over at Gabe's house so much that I became a regular fixture in their life.

We quickly learned that we were similar in our knowledge of tractors and row cropping. We spent our free time reading farming trade magazines and drawing pictures of tractors and farmer's rigs. Some days, when the tractors weren't being used, we would get on them and pretend we were driving them in the field. The two of us, in our play, pretended that we were working.

Our conversation eventually came to the subject of religion. I discovered that Gabe and his family went to the same denomination as the Chafins. As soon as I found out, I said, "Hey, I'm going to church with you!" I don't remember exactly how it went down. I don't know who initiated it, but it didn't take long, and I was planning to go to church with the Moudys.

I decided that I wanted to be like Jacob, not Esau. I was called to be about my Father's business at an early age. Since Odessa, I had been praying for a godly father. In addition, I had prayed for my family to go to church, have a mom and dad, and live in a house with a foundation and not a skirt. With the Moudys, I tasted everything I had prayed for. My heart was joyful because all these things were coming together for the first time.

* * *

When I told the Moudys I was interested in attending church with them, Mr. Moudy came over and talked to Granny Marge and Papa Bill. He didn't want to be just some random creepy guy who came over, picked up the kid, and took him to church.

Granny Marge and Papa Bill agreed that a little church couldn't hurt. They had seen a few of my angry outbursts and bad decisions. They thought, "You know, if anybody needs a little bit of church, I think it might be Matt!"

My mother remained transient and struggled to make ends meet over the next few years. Luckily, we stayed in the Lubbock area near the Moudys most of this time. They were always willing to give up their extra gas and time to pick me up on the way. It was never on the way for them, but they made it work. The Moudys loved watching us play and knew it was a special friendship.

I went with them every time the church doors were open. We played after church with all the other kids while the grown-ups stood around and talked. If the Moudys went out to eat, I went out to eat. If there was some event at church, they included me and paid my way. For every function of the church, I was there. I loved every minute of it.

I still prayed daily that Yahuah would send me a good, strong father for Mom and me. I wanted a dad to help provide for us and take us to church. Little did I realize then that it was all happening for me, just the way I prayed. Yahuah had heard me and was answering me.

A kid's faith is powerful. Anything is possible when you see an enthusiastic child dedicated to something that aligns with Yahuah's will.

I also prayed for my mother to return to her faith. My mother had grown up going to church. I longed for her to have a fire rekindled in her and want to return to church. I prayed that she would attend church with me again.

* * *

That eventually did happen, making my little heart happy. I thought my world had all lined up, and everything would be perfect. Unfortunately, some events in the church are not perfect. My mother found herself in the middle of a church political battle. I don't know the details, but I know that a young man she was interested in got disfellowshipped from the church. After that, she was disenfranchised and wanted no part of the church again. Fortunately, I was not fazed by any of that. I continued to love every second of being at church.

Once again, Yahuah set my mom up to be like Jacob. She had the example and support of the Moudys and found a church family. She didn't like the discipline of the church. She left Jacob's path and found the path of Esau once again.

The Joy Bus

Idalou was not known for its great wealth. It was considered a working community. People with a lot of money didn't live in Idalou. They lived in other places, and the church in Idalou was blessed to have some very wealthy farmers who believed strongly in supporting the church. They eventually pooled enough money to buy an old school bus.

They painted it white, lettered the phrase "Joy Bus," installed a PA system, and found a bus driver. Alvin got involved and would ride along. He didn't have to pick me up to take me to church during this time. He had the Joy Bus pick me up. On the bus, we would sing church songs. It was a blast! Not long after the Joy Bus came into being, some trouble began to brew at the church.

Some of the issues my mother had seen at the church became noticeable to others. The Moudys decided it was time to leave when they realized it was not a safe environment to raise their children. The Moudys treated me as if I were one of theirs. As we explored new churches, they included me with them. I didn't care what church we went to as long as it was with them. Little did I know that I was living out the book of Ruth.

But Ruth answered, "Don't force me to leave you. Don't make me turn back from following you. Wherever you go, I will go, and wherever you stay, I will stay. Your people will be my people, and your Elohim will be my Elohim. Wherever you die, I will die, and I will be buried there with you. May Yahweh strike me down if anything, but death separates you and me! Ruth 1:16-17

That's how I felt about it. The Moudys continued to drive out of their way to take me to church. The Moudy car became the Joy Bus.

I spent hours riding in the car as a captive audience with the Moudys. It became my classroom, and I had a front-row seat to being a part of a family and instructed by a loving father. The entire Moudy family was a good example of a father, friend, and spiritual leader that my children would need.

Without these car rides, I don't know if I would have had the skills I needed later in life. I saw what it was like having three kids. Gabe and Robyn had another sister that came along around the time when I met them. Since we played outside, it took a while for me to meet Lynsey. She was much younger than the rest of us, and I didn't have much interaction with her when she was a baby. Lynsey never really knew life without me. To her, I was her older brother.

Grafted In

When the Moudys visited their grandparents in Happy and Lazbuddie, they would invite me to go with them. The Moudys and the Mimms never treated me like a stranger. They always welcomed me into their home like a grandchild. They grafted me into their respective tribes.

Alvin and Mary Moudy lived in Happy, Texas. Happy is "the town without a frown!" Happy is north of Lubbock and south of Amarillo. It wasn't too far of a drive from our home in Lubbock, and I always thought it was fun. The Mimms lived further west near Lazbuddie, Texas.

Both sets of Grandparents were very influential in their community, church, and school. They searched the scriptures daily and sought to live their life as laid out in the bible. They were both Elders in their local church. Gramps was a high school principal, physics and biology teacher by day, and farmer on the nights and weekends. Grandy (Mary Moudy) was a watercolor artist. Grandy spent most of her free time painting and doing things with her grandchildren.

I called them Mr. and Ms. Moudy early on, but that just got confusing because nobody knew who I was talking about. Alvin Moudy Senior and Mary Moudy finally said, "Call us Gramps and Grandy, please." That made me feel like I was one of them. The entire Moudy clan called me an honorary Moudy. Today, I'm honored and incredibly grateful to be a part of that heritage. It was a lineage vastly different from mine, one of successful marriages and a commitment to faith.

I also would go to Jill's parents in Lazbuddie, Texas. It was out on the western edge of the panhandle near New Mexico. Lazbuddie was a very tiny town made up of a handful of farmers. I called them Mr. and Mrs. Mimms. It didn't take long for them to tell me, "Matt. Please call us Grandmother and Granddad. That's what our grandchildren call us and what we want you to call us." Pete and Bobby Mimms had a lifelong marriage and children who were kingdom-minded. Pete was as hardworking as my Grandfather Carl.

Pete and Bobby also made me feel comfortable being at their home. They made me feel like I was one of their own. Pete was a larger-than-life kind of man. He was a "Jack of All Trades" and mastered most of them. But most importantly, he loved to sit around the table, tell bible stories, and sing with his grandkids. Pete enjoyed seeing young folks interested in farming and church. It made his day that Gabe had a friend interested in farming practices. He believed that everyone needed to work hard. Pete wanted to see more kids get involved in farm life. He would find ways to get us involved. He thought everyone needed to get their hands dirty with work. Pete's life was filled with family, working hard, and attending church.

Amazingly, the Moudys and the Mimms were God-fearing farmers who put their family above their interests. The Chafins, Moudys, and Mimms were all members of the Church of Christ who diligently studied Yahuah's Word. They loved His Word and delighted in His ways. I was drawn to them. I knew the world's ways and knew it was no good. I wanted to be around the Chafins, Moudys, and Mimms.

Many nights, I had cried myself to sleep. I cried out to Yahuah, begging him to send me a godly dad. Not only did he give me a godly parent in the Moudys, but he gave me two different sets of Grandparents who adopted me as one of theirs. They were the first to show me that family is more than a bloodline.

Yahuah tripled the blessing for me. I asked for one dad, and He gave me three! He wanted to make sure that I was covered! All six grandparents were happy to take me under their wings lovingly.

He will cover you with His feathers, and under His wings, you will find refuge; His faithfulness will be your shield and rampart. Psalm 91:4

They would have compassion on me and teach me the ways of the Father. They were the same on the farm, in town, and in their home. They were people who didn't cuss, smoke, or drink. They lived out their faith in all aspects of life.

The Moudys, Mimms, and Chafins all practiced Deuteronomy 6.

Listen, Israel: Yahweh is our Elohim. Yahweh is the only God. Love Yahweh your Elohim with all your heart, with all your soul, and with all your strength. Take to heart these words that I give you today. Repeat them to your children. Talk about them when you're at home or away, when you lie down or get up. Write them down, and tie them around your wrist, and wear them as headbands as a reminder. Write them on the doorframes of your houses and on your gates. Deuteronomy 6:4-9-8

It commanded the children of Israel to talk about the commandments 24/7. When they walked down the road, they spoke about Yahuah. They talked about the Word with their children when they laid down and went to sleep. They told the great stories and wonderful things Yahuah had done to His people as if it happened to them and their ancestors. The Moudys, Mimms, and Chafins believed this to be a universal truth. A truth that could not be broken, separated, or changed. They had a conviction that went deep into their bones. A Daniel-type conviction is one for which you're willing to die.

Shadrach, Meshach, and Abednego answered King Nebuchadnezzar, "We don't need to answer your last question. If our Elah, whom we honor, can save us from a blazing furnace and from your power, he will, Your Majesty. But if he doesn't, you should know, Your Majesty, we'll never honor your gods or worship the gold statue that you set up." Daniel 3:16-18

Glenn, A Window Washing Cowboy

My mother met a new boyfriend sometime during my third-grade year. Glenn was a window washer who lived across the street from his parents in a trailer park community a couple of miles south of the Moudy home.

My mother fell in love. She moved us into Glenn's trailer. This was a substantial change in my life. I was excited because I thought this was the dad I had prayed for. Glenn was an outdoors person. He loved to take us all fishing. My mother loved to fish for carp in the local Playa lakes.

In Lubbock, many Playa lakes were full of carp and other so-called "trash fish." These fish weren't hard to catch. They were too bony for most people to try to eat. We would catch and release them. It was something to do on the weekend. We would go out in our 1979 red Ford Pinto, which I thought was the coolest car in the world at the time. Sometimes, she would mix Corn Flakes and Big Red soda to make a cheap doughball for bait. We would sit all day and fish. The day's standard was jean cut-off shorts and my International tractor hat. I enjoyed fishing with Glenn and my mother.

Glenn and my mother were not church-going people. My first memories of Glenn are seeing him after he broke his back. He had an accident, and he fell off a scaffolding. He was unable to work. When we first moved in with Glenn, he had a hospital bed in the middle of his trailer house.

Before the marriage, I remember visiting Glenn wearing my pearl snap western shirt and a straw cowboy hat. Glenn also wore a cowboy hat, and I thought I was in good company.

Glenn and his neighbor raised Gamecock chickens for fighting. They had an arena set up in the back of their house. It was a place for you to bring your roosters to a gladiator-type battle. You would put the roosters in a circle. Everybody would gather up and bet on which rooster would win. It was illegal and inhumane. Contestants would purchase artificial spurs and put them on roosters, enabling them to help kill the other rooster. Glenn would give me money to bet on one of the roosters. Keep in mind I was in the fourth grade. I had no idea this was an illegal activity.

At this point in my life, I started exploring new friendships outside Gabe's. Gabe was slightly further away, and I no longer had my pony. My only mode of transportation was the bike, and I couldn't ride it over to Gabe's because it was too far and dangerous. My mother worried more about me riding the bike than she did the pony. It was here that I met the Sycamore Trailer Park Gang.

The trailer park had a notorious gang of young boys with nothing better to do than harass and annoy anyone nearby. They invited me into their circle and told me I was an honorary member of their gang. They wanted me to be a part of their "Mexican Gang."

Our favorite activity was the "bucket toss." We would stand on the side of the road with a little bucket and toss it under passing cars at the last second. The bucket would roll around under the car and make a terrible racket like something was wrong with their vehicle. The adults would stop and try to figure out what happened. Meanwhile, we would just laugh.

This was all fun until we did this to a younger driver who was fast and could chase us. As soon as he began to run after us, my friends took off and left me behind. I was slower and heavier than my friends. They all easily outran me. I was caught. He chewed me out, took me by my ear to my mom's door, and told her I was spending time with kids that would get me into trouble. It wasn't long after that I had to go back to the gang and tell them, "Look, my mom says I can't spend time with you and be a part of your gang anymore." To which they replied, "You will always be an honorary Sycamore Trailer Park Gang member." Later in life, I realized they wanted me in this Mexican gang because I was the chubbiest and slowest kid.

One night, my mother woke me and told me to grab everything I owned. We threw it in the back of the car and moved out. I didn't see Glenn again until I was an adult with my kids.

Glenn had started strong. He spent time with me, and he loved me like a father. He wanted to be like Jacob but struggled with his identity. When I knew him, he had a good heart and meant well, but he followed the path of Esau and did what he wanted. Of the men in my life who weren't Chafin, Mimms, or Moudy, Glenn came close to being a good man. You see, that is just it. He was good but not godly. There is a difference. Once again, I found myself longing for an intact family. A family that prayed and went to church together. A family that had God first and everything else second.

Dan the Machinist

After leaving Glenn's, my mom was a wreck and needed space and time to work things out. She called the Moudys to see if they could help. They were my rock when times were crazy. The Moudys came by, picked me up, and took me to church. I spent that weekend with them.

My mother trusted the Moudys. She needed me to stay a few weeks with them until she could figure things out. She was going to re-establish herself on her own. She was tired of living with her mother and was determined not to go back. She needed to be on her feet for a while and save enough money to support the two of us.

I found myself homeless again. My mother always provided for me even if she had to admit defeat and humiliation and swallow some pride. She did what was necessary to ensure my needs were met.

My mother had to take a job at Pinky's Liquor Store. Pinky's was located just outside the "dry" city of Lubbock. You couldn't sell alcohol in the city limits. While working at Pinky's, my mother saved up a little money. She moved out during my sixth-grade year and found herself a little trailer. We would still be in the same school district. This trailer was in a sketchy park. She struggled to make ends meet, forcing her to ask the Moudys if I could go live with them and finish the school year until she could fully support us.

* * *

During this time, she met a new boyfriend who loved to eat Pinky's barbecue sandwiches and was always getting in her line. Dan was a retired Navy Veteran who was working as a machinist. They began to date, and my mother was getting close to husband number three.

Soon Dan asked her to marry him, and she said yes. They asked me if I wanted to go to the wedding, to which I replied, "No, not really. I don't want to go." I was not a fan of Dan.

Much to my amazement, they said, "Okay, you don't have to go." The Moudys took me that weekend and kept me busy. I didn't like the thought of Dan from the beginning. I was old enough now to have an impression of people. He was not what I would have considered a godly man. I was an "open book" with no poker face, and I am sure that my mother knew of my disapproval.

I agreed that after the marriage and honeymoon, I would rejoin her and my new life with Dan. Dan was a former track star and a legend in his own mind. He stopped running after a motorcycle accident that required foot surgery. Even though he had a lame foot, he was the fastest, fat, bald man I had ever seen!

Dan enjoyed being outdoors. He let me camp in the front yard with his new tent one night. That night, it poured down rain. I gave up on the camping and returned to the house in the middle of the night when the wind picked up. In the morning, Dan asked me, "Well, how was it?" Just as he asked me we saw a blue blur go across the yard. Dan took off running after his new tent, chasing it down in a neighboring cotton field.

My mom had quit the liquor store and was now working at the local convenience store in our neighborhood. It was close enough that she could walk there. She loved her job, and most of all, she loved bringing home ice cream and Butterfinger candy bars for snacking after her shift. This was one of my favorite things to eat with her.

On my new bus, I met Joe. Joe began to bring me my favorite snacks,

Butterfingers and Dr. Pepper. Joe would come over so we could ride bikes after school. Soon after meeting Joe, my bike went missing and was presumed stolen. Dan happened to be home when he saw Joe riding around on my bike! Speedy Dan ran after Joe and chased him down. He caught up with Joe and took the bike from him. That day, I learned a valuable lesson about people who try to buy your friendship.

VBS and the Police

In the summer of my sixth-grade year, the Chafins invited me to the Knox City Church of Christ Vacation Bible School, and I stayed with them for several weeks. When I left for Knox City, we all understood I would stay at the farm for some time like I usually did in the summers. I was ecstatic to get to go and be with my Grandpa and Grandma. Once I got to Knox City, I went everywhere Grandpa went. The local shop owners called me his "right-hand man" which made me very proud.

I was at VBS every day. It was a week full of food, bible, and fun. They taught me about the love of Jesus and a love for His Word.

We went back to do the normal chores on the cotton farm the day VBS was over. We headed into the house to change into our work clothes. As we walked into the house, the phone rang. Grandma Hank answered and got noticeably quiet and somber. As the conversation continued, I could tell that something was not right. She quietly hung up the phone and called Carl into the other room. Then I heard some strong whispering as they discussed the phone call.

They entered the living room within minutes and said, "Matt, we must take you back to Lubbock right now." I was shocked and couldn't understand. How could my summer come crashing down so suddenly? At first, I was filled with sadness, which soon turned into anger. I was angry about having to cut my summer short with my grandpa. I wanted nothing more in the world than to be with him. I was forced to return to my mother and Dan, whom I loathed.

At 12 years old, there was nothing that I could do about this situation but get in the car and enjoy the last moments with my grandparents. It was a quiet trip back to Lubbock. As we pulled up to the green and white trailer I called home, I noticed a police car in the driveway. I saw my Granny Marge and my mother talking to the police. I thought that was odd, and I wondered what was happening. We parked in the driveway behind the police car. The officer approached my grandpa and said, "I'm Officer Trevino. I assume you are Mr. Carl Chafin. Is that correct?" Carl said, "Yes, sir, it is." Then the officer said, "Well, Mr. Dan Paul has requested that you return his child to him immediately, and we appreciate you getting him to Lubbock as fast as you could." My Grandfather was a very compliant man and was not trying to cause problems with anyone. He quickly responded, "Matt, you need to get out of the car and go with your mom now." I can remember being upset and in tears. I ran into my room and cried myself to sleep, refusing to come out for dinner that night. My grandparents drove away, devastated that our time was cut short.

Jacob adopts his grandkids as his own and redeems them from a pagan land. While Joseph was considered righteous, he married the daughter of a "priest of On." Not much is known about her and what she believed. It seems logical that Jacob redeemed the children so they could be raised in the proper God-fearing environment. What my Grandfather Carl wanted to do was be like Jacob. Carl knew his great-grandchild was growing up in a home that was "out of covenant." As a farmer, Carl understood the parable of the sower. He knew it was his job to plant seeds of the Kingdom in my heart. He knew that God promised to give the increase if he did his part.

So your two sons, who were born in Egypt before I came here, are my sons. Ephraim and Manasseh will be mine, just as Reuben and Simeon are. Any other children you have after them will be yours. They will inherit the land listed under their brothers' names. As I was coming back from Paddan, Rachel died in Canaan when we were still some distance from Ephrath. So I buried her there on the way to Ephrath" (that is, Bethlehem).

Genesis 48:5-7

Dan's pride blinded him from seeing the kingdom my Great-grandparents were trying to instill. I felt like I was snatched away from what I was supposed to be doing and thrown back into a den of debauchery. From then on, I prayed daily that I could be removed from this environment. I prayed that Dan would be arrested for drugs. I ran many scenarios through my mind and seriously considered calling the police to get them busted for growing marijuana.

Help & Prayers

When the summer ended, Grandma Hank would always insist that we go back to school shopping. She would take me to Dillard's, Anthony's, or JCPenney because she wanted me to feel good about myself and not be embarrassed that we were poor. She ensured I had a new pair of shoes, pants, and nice shirts. She thought every good church-going boy needed a good suit to look his best before the Lord at church. It wasn't just Hank; Carl also always wore a suit to church. Carl even dressed nicely to do farm work. He didn't wear ratty old T-shirts; he wore nice-looking green Dickies work pants and button-down shirts daily. He took pride in his appearance and thought you should always look your best.

My mother and Dan had a little extra money to buy school clothes. We were limited to shopping at Goodwill and getting "hand-me-downs." Hank and Carl knew this, and by the end of the summer, they took another trip up to Lubbock. Dan had already "laid down the law" that we could not take any charity from the Chafins.

My mother found a way to sneak me out of the house so I could meet up with Hank and Carl. Hank's sister Kitty lived in Lubbock, and my mother took me to see Kitty. Which also happened to be where Hank and Carl were staying. I could spend the night with them and then go to church with Aunt Kitty at Broadway Church in Lubbock. After we had burgers for lunch, they snuck me away and went to Anthony's to get my new school clothes. When it was time to return home, my mom helped us get the new clothes past Dan.

I grew increasingly frustrated at my situation. I was tired of living in a family culture I knew wasn't right. I had a father figure that was not trying to live righteously. I cried out for God to rescue me by sending a father who loved God first, cared for my mother and me, and could show me how to be a man. I became determined that I would not follow in the Esau-like steps of my Grandfather, but I knew that someone would have to show me the proper way to be a man of God.

At the time, I thought this meant I would return to my grandparents and Knox City. That was my dream. I wanted to grow up to be a farm boy from Knox City. The Chafin farm represented the "promised land" to me. The Chafins were a powerful witness of a godly marriage. I knew that if I continued to stay in Dan's house, I would not learn what I needed to know.

God listened to me just like He did when the children of Israel cried out to him for help in Egypt. His timeline differed from mine, and I struggled to understand that. I was looking for an immediate answer.

I was looking for a spiritual father who could turn our family around. I was longing for what I had seen in the Moudy family. My life felt chaotic, and theirs seemed stable and calm. When I was with them, I had peace. There was a righteous order to their family.

The Moudys stayed in my life, answering the prayer for me. They continued to drive out of their way and pick me up. They were always watching what was happening in my life. Little did I know their hearts grieved to watch me become so upset with my situation.

In the fall of 1984, Alvin came to talk to my mom. My mom had called him to ask me how to break some news. I walked into the living room and saw my mother red-eyed, and Alvin looked very concerned. I knew something was up. "Matt," Alvin said, "I am so sorry to let you know," Just then, I saw my mom collapse, sobbing. I swelled up in tears. I had no idea why, but when you see your mom go down in tears, it does something to you. Alvin continued, "Matt, I am sorry to tell you that your Grandpa has died." I was beyond devastated.

Losing my great-grandfather was the first step in preparing me to be a man. I faced the decision to keep going like Grandpa or to be mad and bitter that God had taken away the only flesh and blood father figure I had. This left a big hole in my heart and big shoes for Alvin to fill. Alvin would go on to step up and help fulfill that role for me.

New House

It took a little while for us to realize the trailer house was too small for our growing needs. Dan and my mother began to look for a new place. They found a place out in the country on a one-acre parcel. I loved this house. It had corrals in the backyard and plenty of room for me to farm. It seemed like my life was headed in the right direction! The summer of my seventh-grade year, I had my biggest garden. I absolutely loved it. I was in control of the things that got planted. It was my space, and I could do whatever I wanted. The Moudys came over with a little tractor, and we plowed it up and planted oats so the pony would have something to graze on during the winter months. Gardening became a passion in my life.

As I grew older, my mom would leave me home alone for long periods after school. I had my key and let myself in. This new house had multiple storage buildings. After school, I began exploring all the buildings. I was a curious boy and wanted to know about our different buildings. There was one building that had a padlock on it. I thought, "That's strange. Why does it have a padlock on it?" The door didn't quite latch correctly, so I was able to get down on the ground and peered underneath the door. I noticed there were lights on during the day. I pried open the door at the base and looked as high up into the building as I could, and I discovered that it was full of grow lights, trays, and marijuana plants. I also noticed that a man came by about once a week, rolled a joint, and smoked it with my parents. They had scales and zip-lock bags. They would measure the Marijuana into the bags and sell it to Chuck. I soon began to put two and two together and realized that my parents were dealing. They had a full-on operation of growing and selling Marijuana to a distributor.

My prayers continued. I would ask Yahuah to remove me from this situation. I knew this was wrong, and I prayed and pleaded with Him to rescue me. I wanted them to get busted for their drug use and drug dealing. Little did I know how small-time they were. I never called the police, but I dreamed of it often.

The Moudys continued to drive out of their way to take me to church. Wherever we moved, the Moudys found a way to get me. The Moudys adjusted their lifestyle to help me. They bought more fuel-efficient cars to transport me to church. We were all older now and part of a Youth Group. This meant more driving for the Moudys. They forsook their church attendance to ensure we all got where we needed to be.

By the time I was in seventh grade, I was incredibly involved in the Broadway Youth. It was a bunch of teenagers and young adults that loved Yahuah. We loved coming together to sing and worship Yahuah. We attended youth classes, trips, retreats, hikes, youth campouts, and many devotionals. They kept us remarkably busy doing a lot of things. A youth minister had no other life but a life of youth events. They made church a lot of fun.

Snyder, Texas

We were fortunate to live at the farmhouse for quite a while. We were there from the summer of my seventh-grade year to the summer of my ninth-grade year. I loved the gardens that I was able to do. Then, one day, it all came crashing to a halt. Dan had found a new job in Snyder, Texas. The following weekend, we went down to Snyder, met his new boss, and saw where he would work. I was impressed that his new boss was a Christian man. I returned to Lubbock with a heavy heart, knowing that my time with the Moudys was drawing to an end. The following weekend, I was over at the Moudy's house and told them what would happen. Their hearts were equally broken. We said our goodbyes and were committed to staying in touch and talking to each other on the phone regularly. Gabe and I said goodbye for what seemed like would be forever.

We had a nice little house in town, Dan had an excellent job and life was going well for him. Snyder High School was the biggest school that I had ever gone to. It was about twice the size of Lubbock Roosevelt. I made the football team just as they hired a new coach. He was the son of the famous Sammy Baugh. He made quite an impression on me. On his first day as head coach, I had incorrectly hung up my clothes in my locker, and he lined us all up and gave us swats in front of the whole football team. That was a mistake that I never made again. He was about six foot four, and when he swung his arm back with the paddle, he could lift you off the ground. One swat from him, and you knew he meant business.

While in Snyder, I met a young man named Scott, who went to the Church of Christ. His family was willing to take me to church every time, just like the Chafins. Scott was raised by a single mom who had compassion for my situation and admired my spunk to reach out and ask someone to take me to church.

Scott's mom didn't always keep up with what Scott did. Scott was charming and could manipulate his mother. Snyder had an open campus so that we could leave for lunch every day. Scott and his friends drove themselves to school. They asked me to tag along with them. Scott and I had no money for lunch, so Scott said, "Matt, I got this. Let me show you what to do!" We went into the local Allsup's and stole cigarettes. He would return to school and sell them to the smokers. This paid for our lunch. The next day, it was my turn to buy lunch, and they took me back to Allsups. I clumsily stole a few packs of cigarettes, to sell them to the smokers at school.

Scott and I would skip both school and church together. One day, his grandma drove us to church. When she wasn't looking, we headed back outside and walked to her house to get her extra car keys. Returning to her car, Scott and I jumped in and joyfully rode around town while Grandma was in church. We returned to the parking lot about the time church was over and tried to put it back in the same spot, but someone else had taken it.

Luckily, Scott's grandma didn't even notice that the car was in a different place. It was not that uncommon for her to forget where she parked. When she got in the car, the radio was blaring. She said, "I don't remember having the radio on." Scott and I just snickered in the back seat.

My time at Snyder with Scott was fun but could have been better for my character development. Scott hung around people who were not godly influences in his life. He didn't have the same desire to seek out Yahuah's ways. He was looking to have a fun time in life.

Gabe and I continued to talk on the phone every week. We also would plan outings where we would meet halfway. My mother would take me halfway between Lubbock and Snyder so we could see each other. The Chafins continued to have me come out to the farm anytime I had a break from classes.

At work, Dan's boss discovered that Dan was smoking marijuana. The boss was compassionate to Dan and gave him some choices. He could help him get on the road to recovery and kick the habit, or if Dan refused the offer, he would be fired. Dan wasn't interested in changing his behavior. This left us with bills and rent to pay.

This was the fall of my sophomore year in high school. My mother contacted Grandfather Henry, who was doing hunting guides in Colorado. He needed an extra wrangler and would hire Mom on as a cook. He told them, "Well, y'all come up here. I could use your help!" I remember that evening Dan and my mother sat me down, saying,

"We're going to the high country in Colorado. We really can't get you to school. We're considering asking the Moudys if you could stay there while we work in Colorado. After the hunting season, we will determine our next move. What do you think about that?"

My heart leapt for joy. That was the most amazing thing I had ever heard in my life. I said, "Yes!" I knew the Moudys would not say no to that.

Of course, the Moudys welcomed me back into their house with open arms. This was a dream come true. I would share a room and catch up with my best friend. The Moudys loved to see me back in their home. My heart felt like it belonged to the Moudys.

I learned what it meant to be grafted in. I was like a foreigner living in a land not known to me. There were many traditions that I didn't understand. Some of it was a little bit shocking to me. I was still happy to be with a family I knew loved Yahuah and His word. They were trying to do things the right way.

* * *

Foreigners living among you will be like your own people. Love them as you love yourself, because you were foreigners living in Egypt. I am Yahweh your Elohim. Leviticus 19:34

I now understand that Yahuah was having me live out this scripture. This was what I was doing. I was the "stranger" among them and learned their ways. Later in life, I would learn the lesson when I reconstructed my faith to see how the truth of the Old Testament applied to my life today.

I would talk to my mother from time to time. She would call and write to me to see how I was doing. She missed me terribly. I missed her, but I didn't miss Dan. This continued until the end of my sophomore year when she told me they would be moving back to Dan's hometown in Indiana. He had found a new job up there, and he was going to go back home. He was going to take my mother with him up there. She said, "Matt, I know you're already in school, and I don't want to mess that up. When we get a place in Indiana and get back on our feet, we would like you to join us up there."

Should I Stay or Go

My sophomore year had been great with the Moudys. The summer came and went. I spent time with the Chafins on the family farm. When I wasn't with the Chafins, I was off doing something with the youth group in Lubbock. Gabe and I were becoming leaders in the youth group. We also worked for Alvin on the farm and earned a little bit of spending money. By the end of that season, my mother began to tell me they had found a permanent place to live. She wanted me to come up there in the summer and finish high school.

She would talk to me on the phone, and I could tell that she wanted me to be there. Everything in my gut screamed, "Don't go!" I didn't want to live with Dan again, but I knew by the tone of my mother's voice that she wanted me to be there. Of course, she wanted her child to be with her. I had many late-night conversations with Alvin and Jill about this. With their guidance and leadership, I decided to do this for my mother. So, I told her, "Yes, I'll come up there. I'll move to Indiana."

The Moudys planned a going away party for me. They invited everyone important to me. Each one had a chance to say their last goodbyes and wish me the best. I felt like a part of me was dying.

Once the party was over, the Moudys took me to Lubbock International Airport. I was excited as I ventured from Lubbock to DFW to Chicago, O'Hare, and South Bend, IN airport. I had managed to secure a window seat, and my eyes were glued to the ground below the entire time. I was fascinated by all the different regions and features of the US that I was flying over.

When my mom and Dan picked me up from South Bend airport, I was excited to see my mom. We both were happy to be together again. The mother-son bond is a strong bond that stays with you your entire life. No one can replace your mother. They drove me to their house in North Manchester. I had a half attic all to myself! It was a sad night. I drowned my sorrows to John Denver and the song "The Bluest Skies in Texas." As a Texan, I missed being in Texas with my family and friends.

I was soon enrolled in North Manchester High School. There, I made the varsity football team. Once on the team, I discovered I had a coach who went to the Church of Christ. He invited me to join them. I quickly took him up on it and found my new church home. The church in Indiana was much smaller than the church in Texas. Everything was smaller: smaller crowds, smaller buildings, and less youth.

Everybody on the football team would tease me about being from Texas. I was not a giant of a football player. I was about 5-6 and 150 pounds. They put me as a running back and a middle linebacker. I enjoyed practicing with those guys and preparing for the football season. I also got involved in AG and FFA and worked part-time at Dairy Queen. My time in Indiana would be short. One Friday night, my mother stopped me as I was getting ready for the football game. Dan was working nights, and she was going to be home that night by herself. She pulled me aside and said, "Matt, I'm afraid to be left alone at night." I could tell that was not what she meant, so I asked her, "What do you mean?" She told me she was afraid that if she was left alone, she might commit suicide.

I didn't quite get it because my sixteen-year-old brain wasn't fully formed yet. I went on and played in the high school football game that night.

The next day, I called my grandmothers. I told them I had to get my mom back to Texas. She wasn't well, and I was afraid for her well-being. On this day, I realized that my role had reversed with her. I was now more like the parent, and she was the child. I remember her telling me, "Matt, I don't know what to do! Please help me! Tell me what I should do!"

We had to have a plane ticket back to Texas, so I told my Granny Marge to purchase two one-way tickets.

Dan had also been concerned by these things, and he was more than happy for her to go back to Texas on this journey with me. He thought that was the right thing to do. I was excited to travel back to Texas and get back to Roosevelt High School.

We went to Granny Marge's house when I got my mother back to Lubbock. Granny Marge was a "Live in Nurse" for Doctor English. He lived in a mansion across from Texas Tech. It was the most elegant home I had ever been in. Each room had furnishings from another country, giving each room its theme. Dr. English was a humble man who had been a part of the founding of Hospice Care in Lubbock. My grandmother was his caretaker. He had a little bungalow that was big enough for her and my mother.

One afternoon, my mother met me at the Moudys. We had a long discussion about my future. She had paperwork drawn up for her to sign over legal custody of me to the Moudy family. She knew she was not mentally capable of taking care of me and was afraid of committing self-harm. She knew that the Moudys loved me and would provide a wonderful place for me to finish my high school career. I was excited about the possibility of my new living arrangements.

I entered Roosevelt High School in Lubbock and Broadway Church of Christ Youth Group as if I had never left. I rejoined all the old friend groups and did everything I was doing before. I fell right back into the groove of my life.

I moved back just in time to take my driving test. Ann took me to the Lubbock DPS, and I got my driver's license. I had my license but no car. Alvin told me that one of his uncles had a nice little car. It was a 1979 Toyota Celica. It was green and in mint condition. They wanted me to have it. That January, we drove to Happy, Texas, to pick it up.

I drove the little green Celica about a month before I mistakenly turned into a pickup truck. I totaled the little car. Because of the impact, Robyn had a bloody nose and was nervous about riding with me afterward.

The Day the Music Stopped

On Saturdays, Doctor English had tickets on the 50-yard line at Jones Stadium, and we would watch the Texas Tech Red Raiders when they were home. This is one of my favorite memories. Sometimes, they would let Gabe go with me.

On Sundays, I would go with Granny Marge, Gabe, and my mother to eat brunch at the Lubbock Club with Dr. English. The Lubbock Club was a fancy eating establishment that only the wealthiest people in town could afford. I met all the old movers and shakers of the Southern High Plains.

One Sunday, Gabe and I did not go to brunch with them. We had gone to church that morning and were going to get my mother and take her out to eat. I can remember Alvin going to knock on the door of the guest house to get my mom. I stayed in the car with the family and made them laugh while we waited. Alvin was gone for too long. I watched Alvin and his facial expressions, and I could tell something was wrong. He had the same look the day he told us that my great-grandfather had passed away. I feared the worst. I feared that she did commit suicide. Unfortunately, my fears were correct. I met my grandmother sobbing at the door. She explained that my mother hung herself with a jump rope in the home overnight. My world instantly came crashing down because even though my mother didn't have custodial rights to me anymore, she was still my mother. Until this moment, I had been able to see her and be a part of her life. That was all gone.

Yahuah had already been transitioning me to be a man. I knew I was on my own and had to figure out my path in this world. The Moudys were there to help me, but I was the only living representative of my family. I was thankful that my mother had set everything in place beforehand. I was surrounded by friends from my youth group and my church. They sang at my mother's funeral. Mr. Stumbo, president of the children's home, also spoke at her funeral. She was buried next to my great-grandfather Carl.

My biological dad, Steve, reached out to me and encouraged me to come to live with him. After visiting with him, I felt that wouldn't work out. My dad was disappointed that I didn't want to live with him, but I know I made the right decision. I had prayed since I was a small child that Yahuah would give me a godly father figure. He had done this. I would be foolish to leave the place that Yahuah had put me in.

Building a Family

I was ready to move on from high school. Knowing I would now become the man Yahuah intended, I enrolled in Lubbock Christian University, where I would major in youth ministry. I left the Moudy home to live at the Lubbock Christian dorm. Lubbock Christian was a wonderful place for me. It was a place where I came out of my shell and discovered who I was. I found that I was funny, and I liked to be the life of the party. I took part in everything I could do at LCU for the first year and a half. In one of my classes, I sat in front of this dark-haired, beautiful young lady. I was mesmerized by this girl who sat behind me in my Principles of Education class.

I soon found out that she might be interested in me. I pursued Keely with everything I had. She asked me to go home with her one weekend because her mother said, "Don't ride home by yourself"!

Her parents had a ranchette outside of Fort Worth in the small town of Azle. I was excited to see their place. I knew about their cattle operation and wanted to learn more about it. When I walked across her living room and shook her dad's hand, I knew this would be my new family. I had found a home.

Once again, Yahuah had heard my cry and answered my prayers long ago for him to send me a father figure. Little did I know that Keely's dad would help fulfill that role for me. He mentored me with building and mechanical skills that I needed to improve. It took three men to fill the void in my heart and make up for everything that had gone wrong in my life.

With Keely, it was love at first sight. We started dating in April 1993, and by December of that year, we got married in Keely's grandparent's house.

I had no idea what it was to be a dad, but I was more equipped to be a father than I realized! Yahuah had sent my great-grandfather Carl, Alvin Moudy, and now Alan Craig to help show me what it meant to be a father. Each one of these men lived the life of Jacob. They each played a different role and showed me something significant about how to be a father.

I can remember the day our oldest son was born. I remember thinking it was strange that the hospital staff let me leave with him! I thought to myself, "I can walk out of here with him? You know I don't know what I'm doing, right!" I had no idea what it meant to have the responsibility of a baby.

While Noah was growing up, we were plugged into a local church. We did everything there was to do with this little church. I was a part-time Youth Minister, and I loved every second of it.

Then along came Chloe! We realized our house was too small when we found out we were expecting her. I had my grandfather, uncle, father-in-law, and church friends help us with the addition. Noah was anxious for his baby sister to be there, and he was extremely helpful. Soon after we had Chloe, we had Micah. By the third time, I felt I knew more about what I was doing.

Not only did Yahuah surround me with godly fathers to help raise me. Yahuah surrounded me with godly men. They also helped me to be the best version of a father I could be. I will always remember words of wisdom from David Bedford. He once told me in a class, "If you don't have your bluff in with your child by the time they are five, it is too late." I took those words to heart, and I put them into practice. I worked hard on discipline when they were little, especially those first three or four years of their life. They had to do their part by listening and obeying.

I read a book that was very influential in my life, Bringing Up Boys by James Dobson. He described the difference between willful disobedience and childlike behavior. That was huge for me. I learned how to separate the two. When I saw my children in willful disobedience, I had to act swiftly to reinforce our rules.

Rebuilding our Faith

After Micah was born, I became a Deacon in our church. Keely and I were there every time the doors were open. Our life was full of business, but it became exhausting.

I found myself worn out by Sunday afternoon. As I began to research and study independently, theology began to change and outgrow what I had been taught. I began to question the Church of Christ doctrine. That made me very unpopular in that church because they held to their traditional denominational beliefs. We started to have conflicts at church. We realized we were causing more harm than good and resigned from our positions. I had no plans on ever going back to church. A group of people from the old church also left with us. Before long, we had formed a new non-denominational church. I was reading Purpose Driven Church by Rick Warren. I was convinced we should apply those marketing principles to this new church we were forming. As we prayed and fasted, my wife was convinced we should not name the church. Everyone agreed, and we refused to have a name and get our 501(c)(3).

After a few years of starting this new church, we realized that we were doing all the same things that we were trying to get away from. Eventually, we concluded that it was time to disband this church. It upset many people who felt lost and were not spiritually prepared to make these choices.

* * *

Keely and I had also started a Wednesday night gathering of young families. Our lifelong friends, Brad and Amy, partnered with us in the ministry. We shared the expense of the food with each other. Together, we thought that under our spiritual leadership as godly parents, we could help mentor other young families. We were sure they could learn how to be better parents by being around us. We wanted to make it as "non-church" as possible. A phrase we often used was "Out of the Box Church." We wanted to take the Church into the world and minister to the people who needed it most.

Wednesday night was food, fun, and fellowship. No bible study, just hang out. This became chaos. Our kids grew weary of the undisciplined kids that ran amok in our home. The other kids destroyed their rooms. At the end of the evening, it looked like a tornado had blown through our house. It got too much for Brad and Amy, and they dropped out to pursue spiritual nourishment for their family through a traditional church.

The people we were trying to help were in different places. We decided to drop our home group for our family's safety and sanity. We had done all we could, and we weren't willing to lose our own family for the sake of helping others who weren't that interested in learning how to be holy and set apart.

Unbeknownst to us, we were like Esau. We were doing it our way. We had made the church what we wanted, what we thought it should be. We had to go through that to understand that it didn't work. We were not making our lives better. In fact, as a family, we all became more worldly than we had ever been. The families we were trying to influence had influenced us.

Keely's parents had also started a Sunday bible study at their house. We decided to start reading the bible from the beginning. We wanted to strip back the old thinking and denominational ways and look at what scripture said. We wanted to read God's words, not man's interpretation.

We started in Genesis. As we read, we got to the passage about the

Passover in Exodus, where the people were told to do the Passover forever. That stuck out to us. We all looked at each other and said, "It says forever. What does that mean?"

We began a quest to pursue Torah and understand what He meant by observing Passover. We started studying the Sabbath and concluded that we were not supposed to work but to keep a seventh-day Sabbath on Saturday.

Our family read how the Bible talked about eating clean. We started eating clean and keeping the feasts while breaking down the old paradigms and ways of thinking the church had taught us. We learned a new way to think and act. Yeshua describes a parable of new wineskins. I never knew what that meant until I deconstructed my faith.

John's disciples and the Pharisees were fasting. Some people came to Yeshua and said to him, "Why do John's disciples and the Pharisees' disciples fast, but your disciples don't?" Yeshua replied, "Can wedding guests fast while the groom is still with them? As long as they have the groom with them, they cannot fast. But the time will come when the groom will be taken away from them. Then they will fast." No one patches an old coat with a new piece of cloth that will shrink. Otherwise, the new patch will shrink and rip away some of the old cloth, and the tear will become worse. Mark 2:18-21

We had to be willing to question everything we ever thought we knew. We had to tear down our old faith and read the bible with fresh eyes. You couldn't put this teaching in the old wineskins. We had to make new containers to hold the teaching we were studying.

Something to Think About

If you are in the middle of a divorce, consider the ramifications and lifelong impact it will make. If you are a grandparent, do everything you can to make a connection with your grandkids and to Yahuah. Don't throw your hands up and say, "There's nothing I can do!" Not true. It's a lie. Don't give up on the children.

If you know a young man or woman without a father, be willing to go out of your way to connect them to godly people. Teach them that God's word is more valuable than gold.

Jacob's name was changed to Israel. When we become Jacob, we become Israel.

Who are you going to be, Jacob or Esau?

A Word from Jill

Once upon a time, a little boy who had been trained to be kind invited our son Gabe to sit with him on the school bus. The two little boys got acquainted and discovered they loved farm life and God. Gabe invited our family to take Matt with us to church, and every time we went, Matt went. If we traveled on the weekend, Matt traveled with us. If we went to friends' homes, they set the table for our three children and Matt.

Matt had his own bed in Gabe's room and spent many weekends with us because life in his family was unstable and unpredictable. Eventually, Matt became our foster son. He married his wife Keely, and together they built a family with their three children, Noah. Chloe, Micah, and Noah brought Megan to the family, Chloe brought Laramie, and Micah brought Kendal. But most recently, Noah and Megan brought this little love to their family and ours! We welcome Shiloh Calvin Cook and are blessed to call him our first great-grandbaby.

The Cook Family Today

Keely and I have been faithfully married to each other since 1993. In December of 2023, we will be married for 30 years. We have raised three children successfully. At the beginning of 2023, Noah and his wife, Megan, had our first grandchild, Shiloh Cook. Chloe and Laramie are newlyweds married on the same property where we were married. Micah is engaged to Kendal and is a student at Tarleton State University.

Noah, Megan, and Shiloh Cook

Noah is a dad, musician, and photographer. Currently in film production: Big Papa Productions.

Megan is a mom, photographer, and registered nurse.

https://www.instagram.com/big_papa140/

Chloe (Cook) and Laramie Sayles

Laramie is a firefighter, and Chloe is a teacher, coach, artist, and blogger at Chloe's Corner.

https://chloecook1013.wixsite.com/mysite/blog-1

Micah Cook and Kendal Hann (soon to be Kendal Cook)

Micah is an artist, fly tier, photographer, university student, and outdoor enthusiast. Kendal is studying to be a dental assistant.

https://www.instagram.com/cook.filmphotos/

About the Author

Matt Cook had a difficult childhood to overcome. With God's help and the help of others along the way, Matt was rescued and provided for. Today, Matt is a father to three amazing kids, one grandkid, and has been married to the same woman for 30 years!

Matt earned his Bachelor's degree and became a teacher in Texas. After retiring from teaching, Matt became a landscape designer. He is also a co-host of a podcast, Sabbath Lounge, with his good friend Jake. Sabbath Lounge started as a place for Matt and Jake to make their daily study of God's Word public, detailing their journey of following the ancient paths in the Hebrew Roots of biblical faith.

Go to www.sabbathlounge.com for more information.

Printed in the USA
CPSIA information can be obtained
at www.ICGtesting.com
LVHW020903010324
773138LV00003B/41